FC Barcelona

Soccer's Greatest Clubs

Brien Henderson

Cavendish Square
New York

Published in 2021 by Cavendish Square Publishing, LLC
243 5th Avenue, Suite 136, New York, NY 10016

First Edition

Library of Congress Cataloging-in-Publication Data

Names: Henderson, Brien, author.
Title: FC Barcelona / Brien Henderson.
Description: New York : Cavendish Square Publishing, 2021. | Series: Soccer's greatest clubs | Includes bibliographical references and index.
Identifiers: LCCN 2019048483 (print) | LCCN 2019048484 (ebook) | ISBN 9781502652591 (library binding) | ISBN 9781502652584 (paperback) | ISBN 9781502652607 (ebook)
Subjects: LCSH: Futbol Club Barcelona--History--Juvenile literature.
Classification: LCC GV943.6.B3 H46 2021 (print) | LCC GV943.6.B3 (ebook) | DDC 796.334/64094672--dc23
LC record available at https://lccn.loc.gov/2019048483
LC ebook record available at https://lccn.loc.gov/2019048484

Editor: Kristen Susienka
Copy Editor: Rebecca Rohan
Designer: Joe Parenteau

The photographs in this book are used by permission and through the courtesy of: Cover Eric Verhoeven/Soccrates/Getty Imges; series art (badge) Onur Cem/Shutterstock.com; series art (field) comzeal images/Shutterstock.com; series art (soccer ball) FocusStocker/Shutterstock.com; series art (crowd silhouette) Nosyrevy/Shutterstock.com; p. 4 PAU BARRENA/AFP via Getty Images; p. 7 Popperfoto via Getty Images/Getty Images; p. 9 charnsitr/Shutterstock.com; p. 10 Quality Sport Images/Getty Images; p. 12 Archivah/Alamy Stock Photo; pp. 15, 32 courtesy of Wikimedia Commons; p. 17 The History Collection/Alamy Stock Photo; p. 18 DEA PICTURE LIBRARY/De Agostini Editorial/Getty Images; p. 19 OSCAR DEL POZO/AFP via Getty Images; pp. 21, 23 STAFF/AFP via Getty Images; pp. 24, 35 Bob Thomas Sports Photography via Getty Images; p. 25 Adam Davy – PA Images via Getty Images; pp. 26, 38 JOSEP LAGO/AFP via Getty Images; p. 27 Maxisport/Shutterstock.com; p. 28 Christian Bertrand/Shutterstock.com; p. 34 VI Images via Getty Images; p. 40 Bagu Blanco/Shuttertock.com; p. 44 Douglas Stringer/Icon Sportswire via Getty Images; p. 45 Juan Manuel Serrano Arce/Getty Images; p. 48 Tim Clayton/Corbis via Getty Images; p. 52 Miguel Ruiz/FC Barcelona via Getty Images.

CPSIA compliance information: Batch #CS20CSQ: For further information contact Cavendish Square Publishing LLC, New York, New York, at 1-877-980-4450.

Printed in the United States of America

TABLE OF CONTENTS

FC Barcelona is a successful soccer team that means a lot to its fans in Catalonia.

1 THE SPIRIT OF CATALONIA

The region of Catalonia sits in the northeastern part of Spain. Barcelona is the capital city of Catalonia and the second-largest city in Spain. On one side of the city, there's the Mediterranean Sea. The rest of the city is surrounded by hills in all directions. It's a city full of beautiful buildings, comfortable weather, and people from all over the world. If you walk around the city, you will hear several different languages being spoken and music of all sorts coming from every direction. On some days, you can hear the pounding of drums and the roar of the crowd at Camp Nou, the home of Football Club (FC) Barcelona.

THE BASICS

FC Barcelona is a soccer team. In Europe and much of the rest of the world, soccer is called "football." Soccer is a sport played by two teams of 11 players. The teams meet on a field called a pitch and try to shoot a ball into nets at opposite ends of the pitch using body parts other than the hands. Soccer first started in the

SPORT SHORT

When FC Barcelona began in 1899, Spain was ruled by King Alfonso XIII.

1860s, when the two sports that soccer is based on—association football and association rugby—split into two separate sports. Today, soccer is played by people all over the world. There are many soccer competitions every year. Some examples are league competitions, national cup competitions, and international cup competitions.

MORE THAN A CLUB

Since its start in 1899, FC Barcelona has grown to become a symbol of Catalonia and a model for soccer clubs everywhere. The club, or team organization, is known by many names: Barça (BAR-thuh/BAR-suh), FCB, or *Blaugrana*. This last name is a Spanish word that refers to the club's colors: blue and red. They're one of the largest, most successful, and most popular soccer teams in the world. However, their motto is *"Mès que un club"* ("More than a club"), and they live up to it.

Throughout the 20th century, FC Barcelona had their struggles. However, they always managed to enjoy some success on the soccer field. Since 2000, they have reached new heights in world soccer. They have won many competitions, such as Spanish league championships, Spanish Cups, and Champions League titles. The Spanish national team that won the Fédération Internationale de Football Association (FIFA)

World Cup in 2010 had more players from FC Barcelona than any other club. The man who scored the winning goal to give Spain their first World Cup title was Andrés Iniesta, a Barcelona player.

Today, most soccer clubs are owned by large companies or millionaires, even billionaires. For example, Italian team AC Milan is owned by Elliott Management Corporation. They own Samsung,

Iniesta (*in front*) fights for the ball during the final moments of the World Cup final between Spain and the Netherlands in 2010. He played with Barcelona for 22 seasons.

Comcast, and many other companies in addition to AC Milan. Chelsea FC is owned by the billionaire Roman Abramovich. FC Barcelona is unique. It's owned by its members: individuals who pay membership fees. Every member gets to vote on how the club is run and who runs it. Josep Bartomeu was voted in as president for a six-year term in 2014.

The organization now includes teams in several sports. Although soccer is the best known of FC Barcelona's sports, they also have a basketball team, handball team, futsal team, and roller hockey team. The soccer program is the jewel of Barça. They have five groups of youth teams from Under-8 to Under-16, with a total of 13 teams in these groups. They also have two Under-19 teams and Barça B. Barça B is just below the senior, or professional, team. These teams compete in the lower divisions, or levels, of Spanish soccer. (Each division is part of the greater Spanish league.) This is where you can see the young players who might one day play for the senior team. In 1988, the club also formed a women's professional team.

SYMBOLS

There are many symbols that represent the club. The most important are the colors and the crest. When the club was first formed, they played under the crest of the City of Barcelona. However, in 1910, the club held a contest for a new design to establish a separate identity for the club. It has changed in some ways since then, but the badge on the Barça jersey today is mostly identical to the design that won the contest in 1910.

Barcelona's crest symbolizes the club and the country of Catalonia.

It's shaped like a shield with three sections. The lower half shows the stripes of blue and red, which represent the club's colors. The upper half is split into two sections. On the left is a red cross on a white background. This is Saint George's Cross. Saint George, or Jordi in Catalan, is the patron saint of Barcelona and England, which is the homeland of soccer. On the right side of the upper half, there's a group of red and yellow stripes. These are the stripes of Catalonia. There's nothing that represents Spain anywhere on this crest. This is because the people of Catalonia see themselves as a separate country from Spain in many ways. They speak their own language and have a history of conflict with the Spanish government. From the beginning, the club has been connected with Catalan identity.

Another important symbol is the club's anthem, *"Cant del Barça"* ("Song of Barça"). It was written in 1974, on the occasion of the club's 75th anniversary, by Josep M. Espinàs and Jaume Picas with music by Manuel Valls. It's played on the loudspeakers in Camp Nou before and after every home game as the players enter and exit the field.

In 1979, the club began educating young players in their soccer academy, or training center, called *La Masia*. It's based on the Dutch model of soccer training, but Barça's academy is a little different. It doesn't just teach soccer. It also teaches values. There are five main

FC Barcelona's greatest players in recent years have all come through Barça's youth academy. Youth players from 2019 are seen here.

SPORT SHORT

Catalan is a language similar to Spanish. It's spoken in and around Barcelona.

values that the club makes sure its young players know and that the club tries to uphold at every level: respect, effort, ambition, teamwork, and humility. These five values define the spirit of FC Barcelona.

There are many other clubs in Catalonia. There are even other clubs in Barcelona. However, FC Barcelona is seen by most people in the country as a symbol of Catalonia itself.

Early FC Barcelona players, shown here, came from all over: Switzerland, England, Catalonia, and other parts of Spain.

2

THE CLUB OF A CENTURY

One of the biggest soccer clubs in the world didn't start that way. FC Barcelona began with a group of 12 men meeting in a gym. For the first 20 years of its existence, the club faced the possibility of closing down several times. The effort of one man saved the club from extinction and started the first golden age of Spanish soccer in the 1920s. In the 1930s, the Spanish Civil War presented many challenges. For nearly 50 years after the war, the club continued to struggle. However, they still had great players, devoted fans, and growing membership. This was also the time when one of the greatest rivalries in all of sports began.

FC Barcelona grew slowly from a small group of men into a club known around the world today. Even though it's one of the oldest clubs in Spain, it's become one of the biggest in the world only very recently.

TURN OF THE CENTURY

The year was 1898. A young man from Switzerland named Hans Max Gamper was traveling to Africa to help start some sugar-trading companies there. On his way, he stopped to visit his uncle in Barcelona. Gamper found the city of Barcelona to be so welcoming and open that he decided to stay there instead of going to Africa like he'd planned. He found work as an accountant at Crédit Lyonnais and the Sarrià Railway Company. He also became a sportswriter for two newspapers. He was only 22 years old.

People in Catalonia had trouble pronouncing the "H" in Hans, so he adopted the nickname Joan. Today, he's still called Joan Gamper more often than he's called Hans. He was a lover of all sports. When he was a teenager, he played soccer for Excelsior Zürich in Switzerland. At one point, a group of players from Excelsior split off to form a new club called FC Turicum Zürich. In 1896, the two clubs came together again to form FC Zürich. Gamper was a cofounder of this new club and the first captain in FC Zürich history.

When he wasn't working in Barcelona, Gamper spent his free time playing several sports, including soccer. He also helped publish the sports magazine *Los Deportes*. On October 22, 1899, Gamper placed an ad in *Los Deportes* seeking people who would like to begin a soccer club with him. The ad wasn't met with a large response, but it was enough. Eleven men came to meet him at *Gimnasio Solé* (Solé Gymnasium), and Football Club Barcelona was born on November 29.

SPORT SHORT

FC Zürich still exists today, playing in the Swiss Super League.

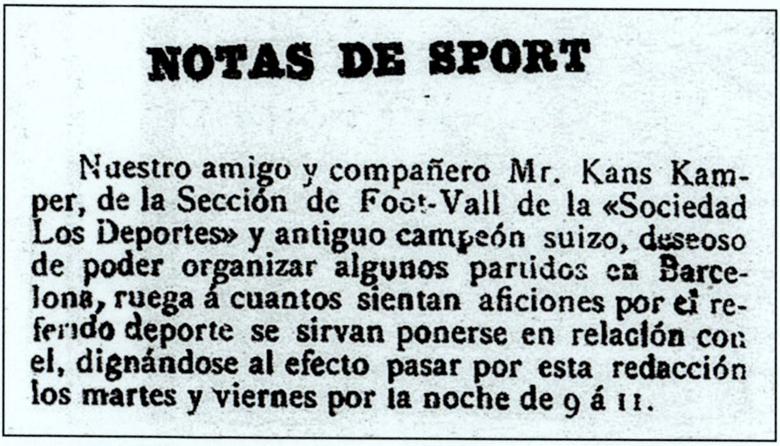

NOTAS DE SPORT

Nuestro amigo y compañero Mr. Kans Kamper, de la Sección de Foot-Vall de la «Sociedad Los Deportes» y antiguo campeón suizo, deseoso de poder organizar algunos partidos en Barcelona, ruega á cuantos sientan aficiones por el referido deporte se sirvan ponerse en relación con el, dignándose al efecto pasar por esta redacción los martes y viernes por la noche de 9 á 11.

This is the ad for players to join the new Barcelona team in 1899. It was written in Spanish and placed in *Los Deportes*.

The other members were Swiss, English, and Catalan. Like Gamper, they were all nonprofessional, or amateur, players with regular jobs.

For a club to succeed, someone needs to take charge. This is the president of the club. Gamper may have been the best man for the job, but he wanted to focus on playing the game he loved. He was a member of the group that ran the club and the captain of the team, but the first president of the club was Walter Wild. He was another Swiss man, and the oldest of the first members. However, Gamper did have a large role in defining the values of the club. He believed that sports play an important part in bringing out the best in people. He wanted to create a club that was open to everyone, no matter where they came from. Just like Barcelona had welcomed him, he wanted his soccer club to welcome everyone and to give every member a vote.

Something else that a club needs to succeed is members. They help make the club money. At first, each member was charged a membership fee. Since the players were all amateurs, the club wasn't very expensive to run, but they still needed some money. By November 1908, the club only had 38 members, and the club was at risk of closing down. Gamper was determined to keep the club going and became president for the first time. He worked hard to raise the membership numbers. After one year in charge, Gamper had increased the membership to 201. After 10 years, he raised it to 2,973 members. This allowed the club to get its first regular home field. During that time, the club shifted from amateur players to professional players. In 1912, an Englishman named Billy Lambe was the first person who got paid by the club to be a player-coach.

TWO STADIUMS

The biggest problem in the early years was finding a place to play. The city of Barcelona was growing quickly. Between 1887 and 1900, the city's population almost doubled from 272,481 to 533,000. Large open spaces were hard to get, and the club didn't have its own stadium, or playing arena, yet. The club finally had its first home field in 1909 at Carrer Indústria (Carrer París today). Barça played there until 1922.

With growing membership and a field of its own, the club began its first golden age. Between 1919 and 1930, the first professional players began to play for the club and membership continued to grow. By 1923, membership was greater than 10,000. Carrer Indústria

Camp de Les Corts, shown here, was Barcelona's second stadium.

could only seat 6,000, so the club moved to another stadium in 1922 called Camp de Les Corts that could serve the club's growing numbers.

WAR IN SPAIN

As the 1930s began, Spain was moving toward civil war. The fighting was between Spain and Catalonia, which wanted to be independent. The war began in 1936, and it ended in 1939. People weren't as interested in attending soccer games during this time. Every soccer club in Spain suffered from the conflict. FC Barcelona suffered from a drop in membership, lower attendance at games, and the cancellation of players' contracts. In addition, in 1930, Joan Gamper died, and in 1936, the club lost their president, Josep Suñol.

Barça was closely connected with those who supported Catalan independence, who fought on the

This image shows the damage done to the town of Granollers, northeast of Barcelona, during the Spanish Civil War.

losing side of the civil war. Several players joined the fight against the Spanish military force. The club offices were destroyed in a bombing attack by the Italian Air Force, which fought on the side of Spain, in 1938. After the war was over, under the rule of the military dictator General Francisco Franco, all symbols of Catalonia and the Catalan language itself were banned. Barça was required to change their crest to make it sufficiently Spanish. They were also required to change their name to Club de Fútbol Barcelona to comply with the new requirements to become Spanish enough for the authorities.

EL CLÁSICO

In this postwar era, the rivalry between FC Barcelona and Real Madrid began taking on the significance it still has today. The two clubs had played against each other as early as 1902, when Real Madrid was founded. However, for many years, the biggest rival of FC Barcelona was Real Club Deportivo Espanyol, another large club in Barcelona. In 1943, Real Madrid and Barcelona faced off in the semifinals of the Copa del Generalísimo. It had previously been known as the Copa del Rey, or Cup of the King, before Franco renamed it. The semifinal had two legs—one match at each club's home ground. The first leg at Les Corts went to Barcelona, 3–0. Real Madrid beat Barcelona 11–1 in the second leg in Madrid. In the minds of Barcelona fans, this was the game that first established the rivalry. Barcelona wasn't just beaten; the team was abused by the fans before and during the game. The referee didn't call the game fairly, wanting to avoid problems for himself from the fans. Fernando Argila,

Barcelona's Luis Suárez (*left*) and Real Madrid's Sergio Reguilón (*right*) argue on the pitch during a game in 2019. El Clásico is always a tense match with lots of great soccer—and lots of shoving!

EL CLÁSICO

Barcelona's biggest rival is Real Madrid. El Clásico games—games between these teams—are always major sporting events, watched by millions of people around the world. They're also usually extremely intense games.

The two clubs are thought to represent opposite political views. Barcelona is connected to Catalan nationalism, while Real Madrid is associated with Spanish nationalism. Dictator General Francisco Franco showed government support for Real Madrid. Most people in Catalonia fought against Franco in the Spanish Civil War.

Even today, conflicts continue between an independence movement in Catalonia and the central government in Madrid. These conflicts are represented during games by the fans, who hang banners and wave flags with political messages on them.

the reserve goalkeeper on that day, said, "There was no rivalry. Not, at least, until that game."

The dominance in Spanish soccer of these two clubs means that they have faced each other several times in key games. They are the clubs with the most wins

SPORT SHORT

Camp Nou was built in 1957.

in Spanish history. Today, any game between the two teams is called El Clásico. At first, it was only used when the two met in the Spanish Championship.

Although Real Madrid was clearly the favored team by Franco, Barcelona managed to enjoy some success under his rule. The arrival of player László Kubala in 1951 marked a great era of winning for Barcelona. Kubala came from Hungary and introduced new playing techniques that surprised everyone, such as curling the ball. He was a quick and skillful dribbler, and he was known for his accuracy on free kicks. He played for Barcelona for 10 years, scoring 280 goals in 345 appearances. A fan poll in 1999 named him the best player ever to play for the club. This was, of course, before a beloved player named Lionel Messi joined the team, though. Kubala had a part in winning four league and four Copa del Rey trophies.

Hungarian player László Kubala (*right*) joined FC Barcelona in 1951 and helped the team start winning after years of losing to Real Madrid.

During the Kubala era, membership doubled, and the team found a new stadium at Camp Nou, the current home of FC Barcelona. When it was first built, it could hold 99,053 people. It has since been expanded to seat 99,354. Plans are currently underway to modernize and expand Camp Nou again under the name *Espai Barça* (Barça Space).

The government of Franco continued to clamp down on FC Barcelona through the 1950s and 1960s. However, the election of Agustí Montal Costa as club president in 1969—and the aging of Franco—began a change. Montal launched a program of recovering the club's lost history, starting with changing the name back to Fútbol Club Barcelona instead of the Spanish Club de Fútbol Barcelona. The name was officially changed back after Franco's death in 1975.

THE CRUYFF REVOLUTION

In 1973, FC Barcelona made perhaps the greatest signing in club history, that of Johan Cruyff. At the time, he was an exciting forward from the Netherlands. Since then, he has become the most important icon from the club's past after Joan Gamper. Cruyff had played for Dutch club AFC Ajax for nine years, winning the Dutch league in six of them. He was on the famous 1974 national team that became runners-up in the FIFA World Cup. This team played "total football." This is a tactic that asks every player to be able to attack, defend, possess, and move together as one unit. In his first year with Barcelona, 1973–1974, Cruyff helped the team win their first La Liga title in 14 years, defeating Real Madrid 5–0 in Madrid. La Liga is the name of the

Johan Cruyff (*left*) became an invaluable addition to the FC Barcelona team as both a player and a manager.

Spanish soccer league. In five years with Barcelona, he scored 48 goals and brought new energy to the team.

Cruyff brought total football to Barcelona in 1988 when he returned to Barcelona as manager. He assembled a team and organized a playing style and formation that brought Barça their first European Cup, now known as the Champions League, in 1992.

Cruyff began a revolution at FC Barcelona, and not just on the playing field. In 1979, while still a player, he suggested to the president of the club, Josep Nuñez, that they should start a training academy similar to what they had in the Netherlands. Within moments of his making the suggestion, it was decided to open the academy. The famous La Masia was born. By the time Cruyff returned to manage in 1988, the youth team had produced some great players. One example was Josep "Pep" Guardiola. Cruyff saw Guardiola playing on the Barça B team one day and knew that he would be an important player for Barcelona's future. He was right.

JOHAN CRUYFF'S DREAM TEAM

Cruyff's "Dream Team" won the European Cup in 1992. It was the first time Barcelona had ever won the competition.

Johan Cruyff managed FC Barcelona from 1988 to 1996. He's the father of the Barcelona philosophy as we think of it today. This is a style of play that favors short passes and possession of the ball. He led the team to win four straight Spanish championships and the club's first European championship in 1992 with the famous Dream Team.

The Dream Team was made up of great international players, but Cruyff also gave players from Barcelona's youth academy the chance to play on the senior team. This included Pep Guardiola, who's now considered one of the best managers in the world. Guardiola continued what Cruyff started at Barcelona by managing during Barcelona's greatest period of success to date. He only managed at Barcelona for four years, from 2008 to 2012, but in that time, the team won two Champions League titles, three Spanish championships, and two Copa del Rey wins.

In 1992, Guardiola was a star member of Barcelona's Dream Team. This team was made up of powerful and talented players who led Barcelona to many victories.

LA MASIA

The name La Masia means "farmhouse." It's a real building, with a statue of Joan Gamper out front, that sits across from Camp Nou. When the academy first started, it was where academy players from outside of Catalonia lived. Not everyone in the youth academy lived there. If they could come to training from their homes, that's what they would do. However, a player like Andrés Iniesta, who came from far away, would stay in the farmhouse. In the 21st century, the farmhouse closed its doors, and academy players are now housed in a large, modern

The small farmhouse that sits across the street from Camp Nou was once used to house young players from Barcelona's soccer academy who came from outside of Catalonia.

Joan Gamper, the founder of FC Barcelona, is remembered by this statue that sits in front of the old La Masia farmhouse.

building at the Ciutat Esportiva Joan Gamper. However, the academy is still nicknamed La Masia.

From 1979 to 2009, 440 young players went through La Masia. About half of them were from Catalonia, and the other half from elsewhere in Spain, with a few others coming from countries like Senegal, Cameroon, Brazil, and Argentina. Not many of those players made it to the professional team, though many have gone on to good careers in the sport. One of those La Masia players who came from Argentina was Lionel Messi. He was just 13 years old when he came to Barcelona.

Guardiola returned to manage Barça in 2008. He stayed for four years. Guardiola developed total football into his own tactical idea, called *juego de posición* (positional play). This idea of how to play the game has to do with positioning and activity, both on and off the ball. Another aspect of Guardiola's team was a style of moving the ball with short, precise passing, called *tiki-taka.* Total football isn't the same as *tiki-taka*, but for Guardiola's Barcelona, the two were combined to create a powerful way of playing the game. Many of these ideas were then adopted by other managers who had great success.

La Masia graduates continue to impress in the 21st century. In November 2012, Barça was playing a La Liga game against Levante. Guardiola's starting lineup had 10 players who had come through La Masia—everyone except Dani Alves. In the 14th minute, Dani Alves was substituted off for Martin Montoya, another player from La Masia. For the remainder of the game, all 11 players on the field were from La Masia.

Many players on this Barcelona team that played against Mallorca in October 2010 came through La Masia.

Barça developed from a group of just 12 men in the *Gimnasio Solé* to a giant soccer club with multiple teams and a room full of trophies. It has been 120 years since the club began. They spent the 20th century moving toward greatness, and finally arrived in the 21st century as one of the greatest clubs in soccer.

Camp Nou is the biggest stadium in Europe as of early 2020.

3 THE TROPHY ROOM

If you visit Barcelona, a must-see attraction is the Camp Nou Museum and Tour. There, you can enter the field at Camp Nou through the tunnel that the players use. There's an exhibit with photographs and interactive videos of the club's greatest moments, a space dedicated to Lionel Messi, and all of the club's trophies. FC Barcelona is a team that's known for its modern success.

EARLY VICTORIES

From its earliest days, FC Barcelona has won trophies, but it wasn't so easy in the beginning of the 1900s. There weren't many clubs, and the few clubs in Spain weren't organized into a league as they are now. These days, FC Barcelona plays nearly 60 games in a season. Their schedule often has them playing two games a week in three different competitions. However, in the early days, there were fewer competitions.

After the club's start in 1899, they only played friendly, or noncompetitive, matches in 1900. Their first

SPORT SHORT

Barcelona's first trophy was the Copa Macaya in 1902.

competition was the Copa Macaya (Macaya Cup). This was a tournament organized by Alfons Macaya, the president of another club in Barcelona called Hispania. It was held only three times, from 1901 to 1903. It was a very local tournament, since all of the competing clubs were from Catalonia. In the first edition of the tournament in 1901, FC Barcelona came in second to Hispania. That year, Barça played a total of seven games in the Copa Macaya and eight friendly matches. In 1902, FC Barcelona won the Copa Macaya. They scored 60 goals and allowed only two goals, winning their final match against Catalá FC by a 15–0 score.

As more clubs began to form, more competitions were organized. Barcelona was in three small competitions in the 1902–1903 season: the Medal of the Spanish Gymnastics Federation, Copa Macaya, and Copa de la Coronación (Coronation Cup).

The Medal of the Spanish Gymnastics Federation was a league format with 7 teams, each team playing the others at home and away for a total of 12 games. Barcelona won the league in 1902, adding slowly to their trophy collection. The tournament only happened once more, the following year.

The Copa de la Coronación was held in honor of the crowning of King Alfonso XIII of Spain. Barcelona played only two games in this small tournament, including the final match against Bizcaya. They lost the final 2–1. This tournament may have started small, but it grew to become what's now the Copa del Rey. It remains one of the three major competitions Barcelona competes in every year.

The tournament to decide the champion of Catalonia was originally the Copa Macaya. After two years of this competition, the name and format evolved to become the Copa Barcelona and finally the Campionat de Catalunya (Catalan Championship). In the course of 36 seasons between 1904 and 1940, Barcelona won the Catalan Championship 21 times.

The Catalan Championship and Copa del Rey were the most reliable of all the competitions in those early years. Other tournaments came and went from one year to the next, but these two were held consistently for many years. They allowed Barça to gain trophies, members, and a reputation.

LA LIGA BEGINS

In 1928, the Campeonato Nacional de Liga de Primera División began. Today, it's usually called simply La Liga. It's Spain's top level of soccer. Teams are matched against each other in competitions throughout the season. The first edition was a knockout tournament between 10 teams including Barcelona, Real Madrid, and Athletic Club Bilbao. Barcelona won the first La Liga, but Athletic Club Bilbao dominated more in its early years. Beginning with the second year of La Liga, the format was changed from a knockout tournament to a round-robin league. The teams played all other teams twice—once at home and once away—with points

The 1928 FC Barcelona squad poses for a team photo.

awarded for wins and ties. Whichever team had the most points at the end of all games was the champion. This remains the format today. There are no playoffs after the season's end.

La Liga expanded the number of teams in the division gradually, finally reaching its current format of 20 teams in 1988. The bottom three teams are relegated, or moved down, to play in the second division of Spanish soccer the next year, while the top three teams from the second division are promoted, or moved up, to La Liga. There are many soccer clubs in Spain. Promotion and relegation allow different clubs to play in the first division.

RECENT VICTORIES

The early 2000s were a difficult time for Barça in La Liga. Starting in 2000, they came in fourth place, fourth again, then sixth. This sparked a major change in the presidency of the club with the election of Joan Laporta in 2003. During his time, the club started winning consistently. He won the presidency by promising that he would get English soccer star David Beckham to join Barcelona. Instead, Beckham joined Real Madrid that year. However, Laporta brought in a promising Brazilian player from French team Paris Saint-Germain named Ronaldinho. Little did they know just how promising he would be. Laporta also hired Frank Rijkaard as the new manager. In the first year of Laporta's presidency, Barça finished La Liga in second place. It was a massive improvement after the previous years. Barcelona hasn't looked back since.

Barcelona's record in La Liga is second only to Real Madrid, which holds the most trophies at 33 as of late 2019. Barcelona has 26, but they've been catching up with Real Madrid. In the 10 years between the 2008–2009 season and the 2018–2019 season, Barcelona won La Liga eight times, while Real Madrid only won twice.

The cause of Real Madrid's dropoff in Spanish titles has to do with their priorities. Both of these giant teams compete in three major competitions every year: Copa del Rey, La Liga, and the Champions League. Real Madrid puts more of their focus on the Champions League, which is a big international competition.

CHAMPIONS LEAGUE

The European Cup was first played in 1956 between the top clubs in Europe. It was renamed the Champions League in 1992. It's the most popular and respected

BARÇA WOMEN

Maria "Mapi" Leon (*left*) and Vicky Losada (*right*) of FCB Femení challenge Delphine Cascarino (*center*) in a game against Olympique Lyonnais.

Barcelona added a women's soccer team, called FCB Femení, in 1988. This was the first year of the women's first division in Spain. FC Barcelona was one of only nine teams. The league now has 16 teams.

The women's team promotes players from its academy the same way the men's team does, and they play the same style of soccer.

Real Madrid currently doesn't have a women's team, so Barcelona has a different rival in the women's league. Atlético Madrid joined the women's league in 2001 and has been a big rival for Barcelona. Atlético Madrid has won the league championship three times, including three consecutive titles in 2017, 2018, and 2019.

competition in Europe. Real Madrid has won the most European Cup/Champions League trophies, with 13 as of 2019. However, Real Madrid has won few La Liga and Copa del Rey trophies in recent years. Barcelona tries to compete equally in all three.

After their 1992 victory, Barcelona had to wait several years for another Champions League trophy. However, more came quickly after winning for the second time. They have lifted the European Cup/Champions League trophy five times in total as of 2019, the last four coming in 2006, 2009, 2011, and 2015. Pep Guardiola managed the team for three of those. Frank Rijkaard oversaw the 2006 victory.

Shown here are members of the FC Barcelona team that won the European Cup trophy in 1992.

The Copa del Rey, La Liga, and the Champions League are the most important competitions in Spanish soccer. If a team can win all three of their country's most important soccer championships in one season, it's a great achievement called a Treble, or *triplete*. Only seven clubs in Europe have ever won a Treble as of 2019, and only one has done it twice: FC Barcelona.

The Barça women's team, known as FCB Femení, has also won its share of trophies. When FCB Femení started in 1988, they joined the Primera División de la Liga de Fútbol Femenino, which is usually shortened to Liga Femenina. It's the first division of women's soccer in Spain. Much like the men's team, FCB Femení didn't win a lot at first, but they had a run of four Liga Femenina titles in a row from 2012 to 2015. They have also won six of the women's counterpart to the Copa del Rey—the Copa de la Reina (Queen's Cup)—as of 2019. However, they have won the most trophies in the regional competition, the Copa Catalunya Femenina (Women's Catalan Championship). In the 2018–2019 season, they reached the Women's Champions League final for the first time. They lost to Olympique Lyon 4–1, but getting to the final was a victory in itself. FCB Femení had set a goal to get to the final by 2020, so they were one year ahead of schedule.

PLAYER AWARDS

Several of Barcelona's players have also earned individual awards. The Pichichi award is given to the top goal scorer in La Liga for the year. Ten Barcelona players have won the Pichichi since it was first given in 1953.

SPORT SHORT

Barcelona's first star player was Paulino Alcántara. He played from 1912 to 1916 and scored 369 goals.

Lionel Messi won it in 2018–2019 after scoring 15 more goals than his nearest competitors: his own teammate Luis Suárez and Karim Benzema of Real Madrid.

The European Golden Boot (or Golden Shoe) is given to the player who has scored the most goals among all of the European leagues. Barcelona players (current and past) who have won the Golden Boot include Luis Suárez, Lionel Messi, and Cristiano Ronaldo. As of 2019, Lionel Messi was once again a top scorer.

Other awards are voted on by different groups. The Ballon d'Or (French for "Golden Ball") is an award given to the player who is considered the best player of the year. It is voted on by soccer journalists. Six different Barcelona players have won the Ballon d'Or, with Messi being the biggest winner for the club, with six. In 2019, four Barcelona players were nominated for the award, with Messi winning the trophy.

The FIFA World Player of the Year is another award given to individual players. This award is voted on by captains and coaches of national teams, along with some journalists that FIFA (the world soccer governing organization) invites to vote. This award was merged with the Ballon d'Or from 2010 to 2015. After that, they

Lionel Messi is shown here with his Ballon d'Or award in front of his home fans at Camp Nou in 2016.

were split up again, and FIFA renamed their award the Best FIFA Men's Player in 2016. In late 2019, Lionel Messi won this award.

The UEFA Men's Player of the Year award is similar to FIFA's award and the Ballon d'Or, since people vote for the winners. It was first given for the 2010–2011 season, and it went to Lionel Messi, who won it again in 2015. Andrés Iniesta won it in 2012. The UEFA Women's Player of the Year in 2017 was given to FCB Femení player Lieke Martens.

BARÇA FOUNDATION

FC Barcelona has a foundation with many programs that promote the values of the club through sports. One program provides support for refugees. Another provides tools to prevent bullying at school. They have another program that gives medical care to children with serious illnesses. The club also supports inclusion for disabled children through sports. The Barça Foundation was named "Foundation of the Year" in 2017 by an organization called Peace and Sport, an international group that's trying to make the world more peaceful through the power of sports.

This a staggering number of trophies for one club to win. FC Barcelona has gone through periods when they didn't win anything. However, recent history has been the greatest period of success for Barcelona, and there's no reason to think that they will not continue to win trophies in the years ahead.

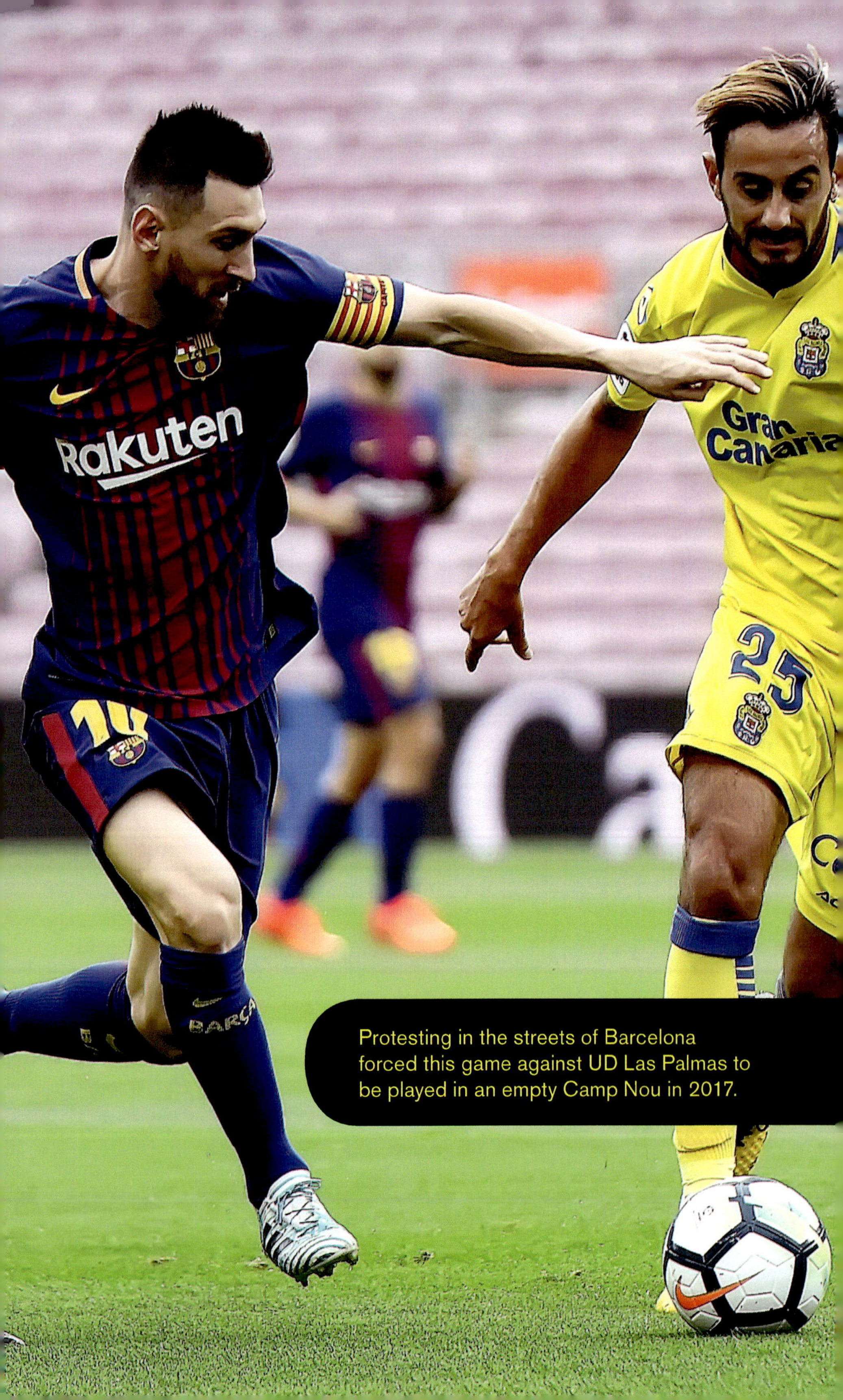

Protesting in the streets of Barcelona forced this game against UD Las Palmas to be played in an empty Camp Nou in 2017.

4

TROUBLE IN CATALONIA

As long as the club has existed, FC Barcelona has connected itself with Catalonia. This has caused more than a little trouble for the club. For many people in Spain, the club is a symbol of Catalan identity. They have been called "the symbolic and unarmed army of Catalonia."

CAMP NOU IS EMPTY

The movement in Catalonia to break away from Spain began as early as 1922, but it continues to be a part of life in the region today. On October 1, 2017, the government of Catalonia held a vote with one simple question: "Do you want Catalonia to become an independent state in the form of a Republic?" The national government, based in Madrid, tried to stop the vote from happening. Several voting stations were raided by national police forces. Civilians and police officers were injured in violent protests all around the region. However, the local police didn't follow orders from Madrid, and several voting stations were allowed to carry out the vote. Over 2 million votes were cast. It

SPORT SHORT
Barcelona has never been relegated to a lower division in Spanish soccer.

was a landslide, with 92 percent voting yes. The Spanish government declared that the vote was illegal.

The next day, October 2, FC Barcelona had a La Liga match scheduled against UD Las Palmas at Camp Nou. With protests and violence happening all over the city, the club had to decide whether to play the match or not. If they canceled, they might have been forced to forfeit the league, not just the game. They decided to play the game but not to allow any fans into the stadium. Only reporters from newspapers, television, and radio were allowed to watch the game inside the stadium. It was played in front of empty seats. Barcelona won the game with a 3–0 score. Las Palmas was not a strong opponent, and yet, it was one of the most difficult games for some players from Barcelona.

CATALONIA CONNECTION

Catalonia's fight for independence has been waged for decades. It has led to many troubling moments for the soccer club. The period after the Spanish Civil War was the worst time for FC Barcelona, since most of the fighters and leaders in Catalonia were on the losing side of the war. However, today, the challenge facing the club is how to stay on top of the world of soccer while still maintaining that connection with Catalonia.

Past presidents of the club have been more vocal about their opinion. Current president Josep Bartomeu has chosen to show support for the right of people in Catalonia to vote on the question of independence without taking a side on which way they should vote. As the one who speaks for the club, he has to be careful. The club needs to keep people on both sides of the issue happy. If they take the side against independence, their fans will rise up against them, and they will probably lose a lot of members. If they take the side for independence, they could be in danger of losing sponsorship deals and suffering punishment from La Liga. They have to walk a tightrope between people on both sides.

Some players are very vocal about Catalan independence, though. None are more vocal than Gerard Piqué. He was born and raised in Barcelona and joined La Masia at a young age. He began his professional career at Manchester United FC, but he soon returned to Barcelona and has played there ever since. He was another Barcelona member of the Spanish squad that won the 2010 World Cup. After the game against UD Las Palmas that was played behind closed doors, he gave an interview with tears in his eyes. He said it was the hardest game for him to play in his professional life. The images on television of the national police forces beating the people trying to vote spoke for themselves, Piqué said.

SPORT SHORT

Barcelona is the most successful club in the Copa del Rey, with 30 titles as of 2019.

INTERNATIONAL COMPETITORS

Paco Alcácer (*left, in the air*) takes a shot against AC Milan in a match in 2018.

Besides the rivalry with Real Madrid, Barcelona's biggest rival in European competition is Italian team AC Milan. Barcelona has played against them more than any other international team—a total of 20 matches as of 2019. Barcelona won nine of those, lost five, and tied six. Their first meeting was in the 1959–1960 European Cup in the round of 16. Barcelona won the two matches they played. They won 2–0 in Milan and won 5–1 in Barcelona, for a total 7–1 score.

Milan has never knocked Barcelona out of the European Cup, but they did defeat Johan Cruyff's Dream Team 4–0 in the 1994 Champions League final.

STAR PLAYERS AND LA MASIA

Another great challenge for the club has to do with its players and the demands of being such a large and successful club. The club has always brought in talented players from other clubs, players who already have a proven record of success. When Luis Suárez came to Barcelona from English club Liverpool FC in 2014, he was already known as a talented and successful striker. However, since he didn't come from La Masia, many of the fans had their doubts about how well he would do, and they weren't going to have much patience if he didn't score goals quickly. Luckily, he has been a great addition to the team. In one of his early appearances, he scored an incredible goal against Real Madrid. That's all it took to get the fans in his corner.

Luis Suárez (*right*) duels with Francisco Román Alarcón Suárez (*left*) during a game in 2014.

JERSEY SPONSORS

When other clubs started putting sponsor logos on their jerseys in exchange for money, Barcelona resisted this trend and didn't do it for many years. The first organization the club allowed to be promoted on their jerseys was UNICEF, a global organization that promotes the rights and well-being of children around the world. The use of the UNICEF logo on the Barcelona jersey was not because UNICEF paid for it. Barcelona and UNICEF have a partnership in promoting efforts to help children around the world, so the UNICEF logo was placed on Barcelona's jersey in 2006 in an effort to lift up the organization as well as the club.

The Qatar Foundation was added as a jersey sponsor in 2011. Similar to UNICEF, the Qatar Foundation is devoted to research in science and education. Finally, in 2013, the club sold a jersey sponsorship to Qatar Airways. The jersey sponsor since 2017 is the Japanese internet company Rakuten.

If Barcelona wanted to, they could hire all the best players from around the world. This is how most of the top soccer clubs operate. However, if they want to live up to the motto "More than a club," they have to do things differently. Ever since Johan Cruyff was manager, the fans and members of the club have expected that a Barcelona team will have at least some players who came up through La Masia. These players stand for the Barcelona way of playing the game. If the club decided to move away from promoting young players from the academy, the fans and members fear that the club's identity might disappear.

Still, Barça has to compete, and they have to win trophies. Managing these demands can be difficult. Even though most of the players who have come through La Masia have never made it to the top team, the expectation is that there will always be a steady stream of talent coming through the ranks. Only 7 players in the 23-man squad of 2018–2019 came through the Barcelona academy. Just one player was promoted to the senior team that season—Carles Aleñá. Before that, Sergi Roberto was the last La Masia product to join the top squad, in 2013. The rest of the team is made up of some younger players who were signed from other clubs and a few big-name signings.

As long as the team continues to win trophies and has a few La Masia graduates in the squad, most fans will be happy. The Pep Guardiola era, where many players on the field were La Masia graduates, was a special time. It was pure luck that so many world-class players had come through La Masia. Most fans understand this, but they still expect the club to produce talented players who will make it to the senior team.

In recent years, FC Barcelona has set a standard for success in soccer.

5 THE FUTURE OF FC BARCELONA

Barça is one of the giants of European soccer. This team has overcome obstacles and dominated competitions along the way. Recent history has seen FC Barcelona meeting some road blocks, but the future will likely continue to shine bright for the club.

RETURNING TO THE BARCELONA WAY

In the 2017–2018 season, Barcelona made it to the quarterfinals of the Champions League. Their opponent was Italian team AS Roma in the two-leg matchup. In the first leg at Camp Nou, Barcelona won 4–1. They were almost sure to go ahead to the semifinals. However, Roma won the second leg in Rome 3–0. Since the overall score was tied at four goals, Roma went ahead on the away goal they scored in Barcelona. The fans were heartbroken. It was unthinkable that Barça could be knocked out after getting such a good lead on the other team.

Before the beginning of the 2018–2019 season, the squad of FC Barcelona was introduced to the fans at

Camp Nou. The newly promoted captain, Lionel Messi, gave a speech to the crowd there. He made it clear that one of the top priorities was to win the Champions League that year. The feeling among the fans was good. If they didn't win it, at least the mistakes of the year before weren't going to be repeated. However, it happened again. This time, Barça made it to the semifinals against Liverpool FC. They played the first leg at Camp Nou, and Barcelona won 3–0. In the second leg, Liverpool won 4–0, knocking out Barcelona in exactly the same way as Roma had.

Going into the 2019–2020 season, fans were expecting something new from the club in the Champions League. There are a lot of reasons to believe that the club has learned from these mistakes and is working on improving.

NEW PLAYERS

In recent years, the club has brought in some exciting and talented players. Ousmane Dembélé is a young French player, born in 1997, who transferred from the German club Borussia Dortmund in 2018. He struggled with injuries, but his skill on the ball and incredible speed have been encouraging. Arthur Melo joined in 2018 as well. Even though he came from the Brazilian club Gremio, his ability to possess and pass the ball reminded many fans of two great former Barcelona players, Xavi Hernandez and Andrés Iniesta. For the 2019–2020 season, the club brought in Frenkie de Jong from the Dutch club AFC Ajax. This is the same club that Johan Cruyff came from.

SPORT SHORT

Xavi Hernandez holds the team record for most appearances in all competitions at 767.

There are also a few players from La Masia who seem promising. Since he was promoted to the senior team in 2018, Carles Aleñá has performed well. However, he was loaned to Real Betis in late 2019. Riqui Puig is another product of La Masia to watch. He still plays for Barça B most of the time. However, he has already played a few games for the senior team. His talent is getting a lot of attention, and fans hope that he will play more on the senior team. In a 2019 interview with KOKO DC on YouTube, Puig was asked if he would ever think about going to another club. Puig said, "It's cold away from Barça." He is not just a player. He is a fan himself.

Those are only the young players. Barça still has some of the best players in the world, including the one who many say is the greatest of all time, Lionel Messi. The larger question at Barcelona right now is about their manager. Ernesto Valverde won two La Liga titles and two Copa del Rey titles in his first two years of managing the club. His results were good at first, but the style of the team's play is not what the fans would hope for. They weren't playing total football, *tiki-taka*, or *juego de posición* like they used to. This disappointed many fans and eventually led to his firing in January 2020. He was replaced by Enrique Setién Solar. However, FC Barcelona fans hope that another new manager will come in soon to bring the team back to Barcelona's signature style—and they have someone in mind: Xavi Hernandez.

RETURN OF XAVI

Xavi Hernandez—known as Xavi—came to La Masia when he was 11 years old. He moved up through the ranks of the Barcelona academy and played for the

Xavi Hernandez (*center*) takes part in his farewell match, which was the last game of La Liga, on May 23, 2015.

senior team from 1998 to 2015. While on the team, he won La Liga, Copa del Rey, and Champions League titles several times. He was also an important part of the Spanish squad that won the 2010 World Cup. After his time with Barcelona, he played at Al Sadd SC in Qatar for three years and announced his retirement as a player at the end of the 2018–2019 season. When he left Barcelona, he made it clear to everyone at the club, and the fans, that he hoped to return one day as the manager.

The fans will have to wait a little while before they see Xavi managing the team. He will need to train as a manager and gain some experience at other clubs before he can step in with Barcelona. However, it's almost a sure thing that he will return one day. Many of his former teammates have already said that when Xavi becomes manager, he will continue the work that Johan Cruyff and Pep Guardiola did with the club. Until then, Barça will continue to compete under other managers.

CHRONOLOGY

1899 FC Barcelona is founded by Joan Gamper.

1902 The team wins its first trophy, the Copa Macaya.

1909 Barcelona moves into its first stadium, at Carrer Indústria.

1910 The team wins its first Copa del Rey trophy.

1922 Barcelona moves to its second stadium, at Les Corts.

1929 FC Barcelona wins the first edition of La Liga.

1936 The Spanish Civil War begins.

1938 FC Barcelona headquarters is bombed by the Italian Air Force. The club is forced to change its name to Club de Fútbol Barcelona.

1939 The Spanish Civil War ends.

1943 Real Madrid defeats FC Barcelona 11–1 in the Copa del Rey semifinals.

1957 Camp Nou opens.

1973 Johan Cruyff joins FC Barcelona from AFC Ajax.

1974 The team wins its first La Liga title in 14 years with Johan Cruyff.

1979 La Masia training academy is founded.

1988 Johan Cruyff becomes manager.

1992 The team wins its first European Cup trophy with the "Dream Team."

2008 Josep "Pep" Guardiola becomes manager.

2009 Barcelona wins its first Treble under Guardiola.

2015 Barcelona wins its second Treble under manager Luis Enrique.

2017 Ernesto Valverde becomes manager.

2018 Carles Aleñá is promoted to the senior team.

2019 Star Barcelona player Xavi Hernandez retires from playing soccer. Lionel Messi makes his 700th appearance for the club.

GLOSSARY

Catalonia An autonomous region of Spain in the northeast, bordering France.

Ciutat Esportiva Joan Gamper The current home of the Barcelona academy (Joan Gamper Sports City).

Copa del Rey A Spanish soccer tournament, also known as the Spanish Cup and for a time El Copa del Generalísimo. It was the Spanish Championship until La Liga began in 1928.

crest A design that symbolizes a group, family, team, or idea; a logo.

cup A competition in soccer; the name of the trophy won at the end of the competition.

FIFA The Fédération Internationale de Football Association, which is the international governing body of association football (soccer).

free kick A kick taken on a soccer field after a foul or injury, with a few players in front of the net; the object is to score a goal from the kick.

friendly A game that is not part of any official competition, a practice game.

futsal A game very similar to soccer that is played indoors on a hard field.

handball A game that combines aspects of soccer and basketball.

juego de posición A style of play that depends on where a player is on a field that was special to coach Pep Guardiola.

La Liga The first and best division, or level, of men's soccer in Spain.

league A group of teams that plays soccer games against each other.

nationalism Dedication and loyalty to a country.

patron saint In Catholicism, a branch of the Christian religion, a holy person recognized by the church as a saint and who is prayed to for assistance or guidance.

reserve A replacement player.

sponsor A person, company, or group that gives money to an organization in exchange for advertising or product or logo display.

striker A player on a soccer team whose main mission is to score goals.

tiki-taka Short, quick, and precise passing; from the Basque language, meaning "quick, light steps."

FURTHER INFORMATION

BOOKS

Ball, Phil. *Morbo: The Story of Spanish Football.* London, UK: WSC Books, 2011.

Cruyff, Johan. *My Turn: A Life of Total Football.* New York, NY: Nation Books, 2016.

Eaude, Michael. *Catalonia: A Cultural History.* Oxford, UK: Signal Books, 2011.

Lowe, Sid. *Fear and Loathing in La Liga: Barcelona, Real Madrid, and the World's Greatest Sports Rivalry.* New York, NY: Nation Books, 2014.

WEBSITES

Catalan Football Federation Official Website

fcf.cat/en

This is the official website of Catalonia's football federation.

FC Barcelona Official Website

fcbarcelona.com

Visit FC Barcelona's official website for all information and news regarding the team.

La Liga Official Website

www.laliga.es/en

This is the website for all competitors in La Liga. It includes news updates, interviews, and articles about the teams and their progress in the season.

UEFA Official Website

www.uefa.com/

This is UEFA's official website. UEFA is the lead governing body of European soccer.

VIDEOS

FC Barcelona

www.youtube.com/user/fcbarcelona

This YouTube channel gives viewers access to all of FC Barcelona's main game highlights and includes featured interviews with players.

FC Barcelona Mega Store

www.youtube.com/watch?v=4DLf1_dL98s

This video follows a father and his young son in the FC Barcelona megastore.

24 Hours at FC Barcelona's Academy

www.youtube.com/watch?v=bcKvEBXcjBw

This video explores a day in the life at Barcelona's youth training academy.

SELECTED BIBLIOGRAPHY

Balagué, Guillem. *Barça: The Official Illustrated History of FC Barcelona*. London, England, UK: Carlton Books, 2014.

Balagué, Guillem. *Pep Guardiola: Another Way of Winning: The Biography*. London, England, UK: Weidenfeld & Nicolson, 2018.

Ball, Phil. *Morbo: The Story of Spanish Football*. London, England, UK: WSC Books, 2011.

Barend, Frits, Henk van Dorp, and Johan Cruyff. *Ajax, Barcelona, Cruyff: The ABC of an Obstinate Maestro*. London, England, UK: Bloomsbury. 1999.

Burns, Jimmy. *Barça: A People's Passion*. London, England, UK: Bloomsbury, 2009.

Cruyff, Johan. *My Turn*. London, England, UK: Macmillan. 2016.

Eaude, Michael. *Catalonia: A Cultural History*. Oxford, England, UK: Signal Books, 2011.

Fitzpatrick, Robert. *El Clásico: Barcelona v Real Madrid, Football's Greatest Rivalry*. London, England, UK: Bloomsbury, 2012.

Goldblatt, David. *The Ball Is Round: A Global History of Football*. New York, NY: Riverhead Books, 2008.

Hanlon, Tim. *Barca: The Laporta Revolution*. Cheltenham, England, UK: SportsBooks, 2008.

Hughes, Damian. *The Barcelona Way: Unlocking the DNA of a Winning Culture*. Audiobook. Audible, 2018.

Hunter, Graham. *Barça*. England, UK: BackPage Press Ltd., 2012.

Jökulsson, Illugi. *FC Barcelona: More Than A Club*. New York, NY: Abbeville Press, 2014.

Lowe, Sid. *Fear and Loathing in La Liga: Barcelona vs Real Madrid.* New York, NY: Nation Books, 2014.

Wilson, Jonathan. *The Barcelona Inheritance: The Evolution of Winning Soccer Tactics From Cruyff To Guardiola*. Audiobook. Audible, 2018.

INDEX

ABOUT THE AUTHOR

Brien Henderson is the producer and co-host of the *Barça Talk* podcast. With a background in journalism, training in audio production, and advanced degrees in music, Henderson applies these diverse aspects of his experience to inform, entertain, and connect Barcelona fans around the world. He launched the podcast in 2017 and was joined later that year by Gabriel Quiroga as co-host. He has been to Camp Nou twice, and his favorite Barcelona player of all time is Xavi Hernandez.